Let's explore Swit

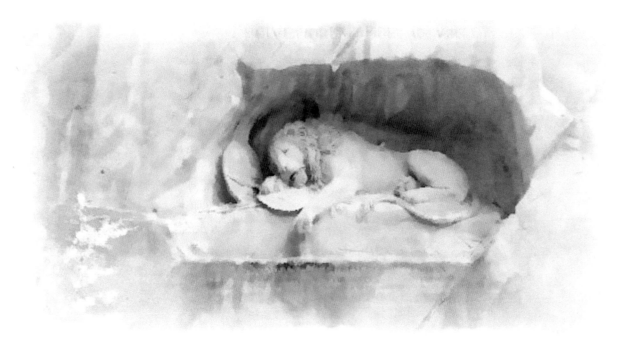

Gurkiran Sandhu

One fine afternoon when I was eating a Swiss chocolate, I thought it will be great if I could visit Switzerland and that's how the trip planning began...

My first destination was the Swiss Miniature. It exhibits Swiss buildings in a miniature form and is extremely fun!

The buildings are created with great detail and they look exactly like the original building.

Next day I decided to visit Lucerne. It is a small city in Switzerland and Chapel Bridge is a main attraction.

Did you know?

1. Most common language spoken in Lucerne is German.

2. Lucerne has many sports facilities such as ice-hockey, rugby, figure-skating, etc.

3. The Lucerne Railway Station is one of the main stations in Switzerland. From this railway station, you can get to almost any destination in Europe.

After visiting the Chapel Bridge, I went to see the Lion Monument. It is a sculpture of a wounded lion and was created to give respect to the Swiss Guards.

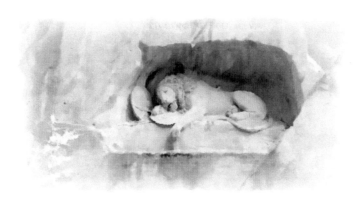

Did you know?

1. There is a latin inscription above the lion saying HELVETIORUM FIDEI AC VIRTUTI which means "To the loyalty and bravery of the Swiss".

2. Mark Twain described the Lion of Lucerne as "the saddest and most moving piece of rock in the world".

3. It was carved in 1820-21 by Lukas Ahorn.

An hour away from Lucerne is a very beautiful town called Interlaken. It is a very popular destination for tourists in the Swiss Alps.

Did you know?

1. Interlaken means "in between two lakes" and it is a town between two beautiful lakes.

2. Interlaken has two rail stations and these stations offer frequent train, bus and boat services to all attractions.

3. It is at an elevation of 1854 feet and can be reached by rail.

The next morning, I took a train to Jungfraujoch, the place I always wanted to visit as a child.

While on the train, far away I could see the meteorological station and I couldn't wait to get up there which is also called the "Top of Europe"

Did you know?

1. Jungfraujoch is 13,642 ft high.

2. It is the highest point in Europe reached by rail.

3. It is very popular because of its beautiful scenery and winter sports.

When I reached at the top, the first thing I did was take a picture with the flag of Switzerland.

Did you know?

1. The flag of Switzerland is Square.

2. It means democracy and peace.

3. The symbol for "Red Cross" was inspired by the flag of Switzerland but colors were reversed.

There is also an Ice palace one can visit at Jungfraujoch. It has nice ice sculptures such as igloo and penguins made of ice.

Did you know?

1. The ice palace was constructed in the year 1934.

2. It is considered the highest-altitude ice palace in the world.

3. The palace's ice sculptures birds, animals, penguins, people and automobiles.

As I was enjoying Jungfraujoch so much, I had to add to the fun by taking a pic on a Swiss Cow.

Did you know?

1. Swiss cow has the second-highest annual milk yield.

2. It makes very good cheese.

3. They are hardy and can survive with little feed.

My final destination in Switzerland was Mt.
Titlis. I took the Gondola ride to explore the
scenic views before I took my flight back
home.

Did you know?

1. Mt. Titlis Rotair is the world's first revolving gondola.

2. It transports you from the middle station at Stand up to the mountain station at 3,020 meters above sea-level.

3. The gondola revolves 360 degrees during the five-minute trip.

Look for other interesting Travel Books on Amazon.com

Let's Explore China, Kids!

Gurkiran Sandhu

Let's explore Peru, Kids!

Gurkiran Sandhu

Let's explore Australia, Kids!

Gurkiran Sandhu

Let's explore South Africa, Kids!

Gurkiran Sandhu

Let's explore Switzerland, Kids!
Gurkiran Sandhu